◆ PRACTICE TO WIN ◆

L A R R Y   J O N E S

TYNDALE HOUSE PUBLISHERS, INC.

W H E A T O N , I L L I N O I S

Library of Congress Catalog Card Number 82-50696
ISBN 0-8423-4887-5, paper
Second printing,.August 1983

◆ CONTENTS ◆

Basketball practice begins each year about October 15 and continues until the season begins on December 1. That forty-five-day ordeal is the most grueling and strenuous I've ever gone through. I know of no sport that demands more effort in the conditioning of its athletes than basketball.

There's a good reason for it: basketball calls for extended periods of going all out, full steam, top speed. What happens when the season starts depends a great deal on how well pre-season practice went.

There are always a few individuals who don't like the discipline of practice, then show up when the season starts, wanting to play. Even if allowed to get in the game, they quickly fall by the wayside. They simply are not in shape and the tremendous exertion of game action soon leaves them blowing and wheezing.

Coach Abe Lemons always told the OCU squad, "You will never play better than you practice." He made a believer out of me.

In high school, back in Kentucky, the October 15 — November 30 practice season wasn't such an unusual strain on us. The reason was that we played basketball 365 days a year. It was a life style for us. Consequently, we were always ready to play.

Some of the same principles hold for living the Christian life. Every day counts in the Christian life. It is not possible to get in the game just on Sundays, then skip all the practices until the next "game." Christianity must become a life style of constant training and conditioning.

For the Christian, his daily quiet time, prayer, and time in God's Word is the practice that keeps him fit. He also learns to share his faith, yield himself to the Holy

Spirit, and strengthen himself through daily worship. With this kind of preparation, he will be ready for the challenge of life.

When the hour of trouble comes...the moment of temptation surrounds you...when life seems filled with the blahs...or an event takes place that makes you ask "Why?" — your reaction will depend on how you've been living your life...practicing your faith.

The disciplined player will face the challenge and come through victorious. The "only-on-Sunday" player may find himself worn down, out of gas, and used up before the contest is over. To play good, you must practice good! That may not be good grammar, but it is true, nonetheless!

So practice to win in the game of life every day. Stay in shape by exercising your prayer muscles. Stay mentally and spiritually alert by drilling yourself on the fundamentals of your faith. When game time comes — when you need the stamina, the skill, the winning strategy — they will be there.

In the pages which follow I've shared different experiences that I hope will not only help you as a Christian but also be of inspiration to you as an athlete. The idea for the book came from the forty-five days of practice that usually precede the opening of the season. As I mentioned above, that's the toughest part of the season.

I would recommend that you read one of the devotionals each day of practice. But it's not necessarily to be read during preseason practice. Hopefully, it will be helpful during the season or at any other time of the year.

My prayer is that God will bless it to your life and team.

Larry Jones
Oklahoma City, Oklahoma

◆ 1 ◆
More Than a Coach

I started playing competitive basketball when I was in junior high school. By the time I graduated from college eleven years later, I had played for some good, and one great, coach.

At times my coaches were mother, father, friend, judge, policeman, disciplinarian, and preacher all in one. They inspired me to push myself when I thought I could never lift another foot or dribble another ball.

They taught me the importance of practice...of conditioning...of endurance...of teamwork...of commitment...of all the things that it takes to make a good player or a great team.

There were times, though, that I thought, *If coach yells at me just once more.... If he doesn't get off my case quick...one more shout, one more yell to hustle, to guard my man...don't do this...don't do the other....If he doesn't lay off soon, I'm going to take the basketball and kick it as far as I can and walk out.*

But I never did, because deep down I knew that what he was saying was not only true, it was also in my best interest, even if it didn't seem to be at the time.

There were other times when his words of praise and encouragement were the most important thing in my life. His "Great play, Larry," or "Way to hustle, Jones," or "Nice pass" could make my week. An important person affirming you is a really nice feeling.

In fact, after all these years, one of the things I value most about my athletic career is the relationship I had with my coaches. I know, though, that this wasn't true for some of my teammates. Some of them flat didn't like coaches.

I can remember some really talented kids who desperately needed good coaching. With practice and discipline, hard work and commitment, the sky was the limit for them. And no one knew that more than our coach. He pushed them, challenged them, and urged them to give it their best. Some took it and some didn't. Those who didn't will never know what might have been if they had only been willing to put forth the effort, to channel their talent, to find the groove.

Then I saw some kids that I thought would never make it. They had rocks for feet and thumbs for fingers. Their bodies went one way, their feet another, and the ball — no one knew where it would go. But they hung in there. They were on time to practice, they hustled, they played full speed with what ability they had.

And soon those rough edges began to smooth out. Their coordination developed, their ball handling improved, and, believe it or not. . . a lot of them went on to become great players. Good coaching made the difference.

A good coach helps a player do what he wants to do better. A coach takes whatever talent is there and develops it beyond the player's own expectations.

That's a lot like Jesus does for us. He doesn't remove the problems or the need for hard work, dependability, and commitment. But he does show us how life can be better.

He doesn't make life simpler or easier. Christians still have the same problems others have. They have to deal with getting along with people; relating to parents; how to treat a girlfriend or boyfriend; sex, money, honesty. . . you name it. All the problems of life are still right there where they were when you accepted Christ.

The difference is that once you have Christ, the church, and Christian friends on your side you have a lot of good things going for you that you didn't have before. Now you have the opportunity to become what you never could have on your own. It's like the coach and his players. . . he helps them to be more than they ever could have been by themselves.

That's the difference Christ makes.

God not only loves me as I am. He helps me to become more than I could ever be alone.

◆ 2 ◆
The Guaranteed Offer

When I was in high school in Kentucky, I was contacted by a number of junior colleges and universities about playing on their basketball teams. I was encouraged and flattered to know that I was wanted — that people saw value in me and wanted me to play on their team.

I remember the good feelings I had when the coach of Vanderbilt talked with me, and the calls that came from the Air Force Academy and from Georgia Tech. It made me feel especially good when Coach Abe Lemons came from Oklahoma City and looked me over. Then he said, "We want you at our school."

The scholarship he offered through Oklahoma City University would make it possible for me to get a college education and still do the thing I enjoyed most — playing basketball. I couldn't believe my good fortune. Not only would I be playing for one of the greatest basketball coaches in America, but I would receive free room, board and tuition at the same time.

That was an offer I couldn't say no to. It was one of the most important offers I ever had.

Life is filled with offers. Each proposition involves a transaction. "You do this for me, and I'll give you that in return." Some are good deals, others are bad.

Each offer requires a decision. A large corporation comes to a young man and says, "We want your services, and these are the benefits we offer." A young man comes to a woman and says, "I want you to be my wife and I offer my love and devotion."

But the most important offer you will ever receive is when God knocks on the door of your heart and offers Christ to you.

He wants you on his team. But the choice is up to you.

Before I received the scholarship to OCU, I had to make up my mind that I wanted to go to school there.

The young man had to sign a contract to receive the benefits offered by the large corporation.

The young woman had to make a commitment and say yes to his proposal before she could share his life.

And you must say yes to God...willingly responding in faith to his offer of a new life. It's up to you to respond.

POWER   THOUGHT

You are so valuable to God that he offers you the best that life has to give.

◆ 3 ◆
Stick to Your Game Plan

One of the worst things that can happen to a team is to get so far behind they have to give up their game plan and let the other team dictate how they play. Many's the time at the half when one of my coaches had to say, "Fellas, if you will stay with the game we can pull this out. Don't let them slow down the pace. Keep the pressure on them. Force them to go for it, to hurry their shots. But whatever you do, don't let up on the pressure. Once we do that the game's gone down the tube."

And sure enough, we would go back out onto the court, down by ten or more, but determined that we were not going to let them slow us down, to get us out of our game plan. When they would throw the ball in we were all over them with a full court press. When they wanted to stand back and give dribbling exhibitions, we smothered them, forced the bad pass or the off balance shot. And when we got the ball it was hustle, hustle, run and gun, keep the ball going, up and down the court, over and over.

Then some magic would happen. We'd steal a pass and race down the court for a quick two. When they brought it back in they were flustered by what had happened. Another quick grab — another two points. Things would begin to happen: a foul, a three pointer . . . and soon they were so off balance they began to play our game plan instead of theirs.

Then we knew we had them. Running and gunning was our strong suit. All those long days of practice, wind sprints, and pushing began to pay off. Little by little our opponents would begin to give us that half step, that extra edge, and by the time the buzzer had sounded, the score had changed and we had won. . .because we had stayed with our game plan and they hadn't.

The same is true in life. There are a lot of pressures in high school and college. Many people would like to force you to play their game. . .to submit to their codes and their standards. When you do, you soon discover that they are calling the shots and making the points. You're playing catchup and without a prayer. It gives you that sick-in-the-stomach feeling to know that you messed up all by yourself. Instead of playing your game and following your best decisions, you followed someone else's.

There are a lot of pressures today to conform to other people's opinion, their bad habits and way-out ideas. But the real first teamer knows that he has to stay with the game plan or soon he'll be out on the bench and the loser.

That's why Jesus offers himself as a guide and support. He never leads astray. He never entices us to do what's not best for us. But he's always interested in our life at its fullest, the plan that's ours and ours alone. It's a plan he designed for us from our very first breath. It's God's plan. . .your plan. Your best shot.

POWER THOUGHT

No one knows better than God what you should do with your life.

◆ 4 ◆
Join the Winning Team

Belonging. . .it's a great feeling to be a part of the team. Walking out of the dressing room and onto the court. . .shooting some practice balls. . .taking off your warmups. . .waiting for the jump. . . . Suddenly the center taps it to you. You pass it off. The play falls into place, and your teammate shoots. . .two quick points!

As you come back down the court, guarding your opponent, you have the good feeling that comes from team work. You belong. . .you're a member of the team.

And so it is in the spiritual realm. God has chosen you for his team and invited you to get into the game on the side of righteousness. Now you have the option to choose him. . .to join the team by being born again. It is the greatest decision a person ever makes.

Here are the simple steps you take to join God's team:

1. *Know that God loves you.* "For God so loved the world, that he gave his only begotten Son, that whosoever believeth in him should not perish, but have everlasting life" (John 3:16).

2. *Acknowledge that you need God's help*. . .that you cannot solve all your own problems. "For all have sinned, and come short of the glory of God" (Romans 3:23).

3. *Know that God will forgive you.* Accept his forgiveness. "If we confess our sins, he is faithful and just to forgive us our sins, and to cleanse us from all unrighteousness" (1 John 1:9).

4. *Invite Jesus Christ into your heart. . .now!* Pray this prayer with me:

Dear Jesus,
I know that I am a sinner and I ask for your mercy. I

believe you died for my sins, and I repent of them now and ask your forgiveness. I am willing to turn from my sins and my old way of life to live for you. Come into my heart now as my personal Savior. Help me to follow you every day, and make you Lord of my entire life, to look to you for the answers I need, from this day forward. Amen.

Welcome to God's family! We're glad to have you on the team. Together with Christ, we are winners!

POWER THOUGHT

As a member of Christ's team, you cannot be defeated.

◆ 5 ◆
Your Goal in Life

As a boy, my goal in life was ten feet above the ground with a net hanging from it. I thought there was no other goal to shoot for.

But the day finally came when I realized that I couldn't keep playing basketball forever. I had to face a new reality, which meant accepting that there were more important things for me to do than sports. My goal had to be higher than ten feet off the floor.

That was a real shock to my system. I had been playing basketball since grade school, had been on the school team from the seventh to twelfth grades, through four years of college, and then went overseas for Venture for Victory. It was hard to imagine not being actively involved in athletics... in having goals that were not related to sports.

But as I kept my heart open and tried to follow Christ, new goals and opportunities opened unlike any I had ever imagined while playing basketball. I married a wonderful Christian girl, went to seminary, pastored, and eventually entered into full-time evangelism. Soon my goals were growing and increasing not only in number but in importance. God began to give me tasks and opportunities more exciting than any basketball game. So much so that I found myself waking up early every morning eager for the new day... ready to look around the corner at what new thing God had in store.

The same can be true for you. God has a plan and a goal for you. It may be something you've thought about for a long time. Or it could be straight out of left field. The important thing is to know God's will and to follow it.

The next question is, how do you find God's will for

your life? How can you have goals for life that are also what God wants for you.

When Jesus was asked a similar question he put it very simply: "Seek ye first the kingdom of God; . . . and all these things shall be added unto you."

I've learned when you work hard at doing your best, other things fall into place. When you're honest and open with others they will trust you and confide in you. When you give of your time, talents, and energy, then God indeed will take care of you. He will add unto you the things that you need.

As an evangelist I've been gone from home for weeks at a time. We have had our problems and difficulties. But through nearly twenty years of evangelism and crusades, hundreds of miles from home, God has kept his hand on us, kept our home intact, and provided for us.

Putting God's will as our first goal is one that works. . . when you're in high school or college, when you're single or married, when you're young or old. There's no greater goal to be realized.

POWER   THOUGHT

Seek ye first the kingdom of God, and his righteousness; and all these things shall be added unto you (Matthew 6:33).

◆ 6 ◆
The Bounce of the Ball

"That's the way the ball bounces."

It's been said so many times that it's a cliché...trite and hackneyed. Yet it's the only way to explain some of the ways basketball games are lost. If the ball had only bounced to the open man. If the rebound had only come off the rim the other way. But instead, it fell right into the hands of the other team. And the bounce of the ball determined who won the game.

The older I get, the more I realize, that's the way life often is. When I was much younger, I basically thought that life would always be fair...that the best team always won...that the person who practiced the most would become the best player...that the referee would always call the shots right...and that my coach would not have favorites.

But unfortunately, life isn't always fair. Sometimes the ball won't bounce your way, the coach may get on you unnecessarily, your teammates may not give you the shot when you are wide open, the ref may fail to see the guy who's jamming his elbow into your stomach every time you go in for a layup.

That's not easy to take. It can result in a bad attitude...a "Why me?"...a sense of always complaining, of frustration and anger. But if we understand it a little better, it may help us to learn to come to terms with life itself...and to understand better what it means to be a Christian.

Being a Christian is not insurance that we will always get the best out of life and receive a fair shake. As the Bible puts it, "The rain falls on the just and the unjust." Good, upright people have bad things happen to them too. But being a Christian is the assurance that in the midst of life's best and worst, Christ will be with us.

That's the test: to be the winning person in defeat, to be the Christlike boy or girl, man or woman, through the worst of circumstances.

P O W E R   T H O U G H T

I can have a Christlike attitude even when things don't go my way.

◆ 7 ◆
Basketball in the Classroom

One of the finest high school players that ever was played only one year of college ball. Yet when he was a senior in high school, every college in America wanted him. He was on everyone's High School All-American list. The scoreboard had trouble keeping up with the points he would score.

As one coach said, "He could do everything with a basketball except autograph it." That was a humorous way of saying he had floated through high school without putting out effort. He could hardly read or write, much less do college work. But as always happens, there are some schools willing not only to bend the rules, but to break them to have a winning team.

One school wanted this young man so bad, that they arranged for another student to take his SAT tests for him. The substitute they chose was too bright and came in with an incredibly high score. What no one knew, though, was that the computer automatically kicked out a score that didn't balance with the student's academic record or class placement.

The result? He was asked to take the test again. The school which had arranged the substitute for him the first time backed out this time and he was on his own. He scored so low he couldn't get into any school. And when the NCAA investigated they ruled he could never play college ball.

But, because a lot of people believed in him, he was given another chance. . . after he sat out two crucial years of eligibility. When he did start, he discovered it was not quite as simple as high school. The league was tougher, the competition rougher. And he was so far behind in his studies that he could never understand what was going on.

By his second year he was angry, confused, and frustrated. He was the epitome of the dumb jock. Back in high school when others were studying *and* playing basketball, all he did was play basketball. He was going to be an All American, join the pros, and make it big. He never made anybody's College All-American list. The pros ignored him. Today he is probably somewhere dribbling his life away.

When you're young and strong, having fun, playing ball. . .making grades seems like the farthest thing from your mind. Unfortunately, some schools take advantage of their players by letting them slip through classes, avoiding the solid ones. . .and even pass up getting their degrees. The reality is that life is not one giant basketball game. Sooner or later, the ball game is over and you have to assume responsibility for a new way of life. If you've done what you should, you'll be ready. You'll be able to assume the load of life. You'll have learned the lessons that good competition teaches: of teamwork. . .of taking instruction and discipline.

As Christians we have a special responsibility both off and on the court. We need to be honest in both our private and public lives. Good things can happen when we do, and bad when we don't.

POWER THOUGHT

We reap what we sow.

◆ 8 ◆
The Perfect Rule Book

To be a successful ball player, you have to know and follow the rules of the game.

Basketball has its own set of rules. The floor has certain prescribed dimensions. The baskets are to be exactly ten feet high. There is a half line on the court. When bringing the ball in after the opposition has scored, a team has only ten seconds to move the ball down court. A player cannot stay more than three seconds in the lane between the free throw line and the basket. He cannot dribble or run with the ball.

There are a lot of rules. To the new player, they may seem confusing and hard to remember. But they serve a real purpose and are absolutely necessary.

Imagine the chaos that would result if there were no rules at all. One team might put five players on the floor, the other seven or eight. One side's guards might tackle the ball carrier, while its forwards tended the goal to prevent any shot from going through the hoop. The offense might hold onto the ball as long as they wanted, then shoot from out of bounds or charge their way to the goal.

Obviously, such a game could never be successful. It would turn into a brawl or riot. It would not be basketball.

And just as basketball has a rulebook, so Christianity looks to the Bible to provide understanding of how we should live our lives. God's laws as described in the Bible are meant to bring meaning and fulfillment to our lives, to give a sense of purpose and order to our living.

In Psalm 19 David said, "The law of the Lord is perfect, converting the soul: the testimony of the Lord is sure, making wise the simple. The statutes of the Lord are right, rejoicing the heart: the commandment of the Lord is pure, enlightening the eyes" (vv. 7, 8). Later Jesus summed them all up by telling us about love for ourselves, for our neighbor, and for God — truly the Great Commandment.

Just as a winning ball player knows and observes the rules of the game, so a Christian is guided by the Word of God. It's not an easy book to understand. It requires study and assistance from pastors, teachers, and friends. But the rewards are more than worth it.

Learn to feel comfortable with the Bible. Memorize favorite sections. Study it until you begin to understand it better.

Here are some favorite verses I've learned and think on at certain times. You may find them helpful too.

When you feel all alone: Romans 8:25–39; Hebrews 13:5.
When you are defeated: 1 John 5:4; Hebrews 12:6–11; 11:28–30.
When you doubt: Hebrews 10:35–37; 11:1–6.
When you need more faith: Romans 4:17–25; Jeremiah 32:27; 33:3.
When you have done wrong: Psalm 35:27; Psalm 51; 1 John 1:7–10.
When you need to get your eyes back on God: Isaiah 26:3; 40:25–31.
When you pray and the answer is slow in coming: Galatians 6:9; Hebrews 12:1; Psalm 27:13, 14; 25:5.
When things begin to go sour: 2 Corinthians 12:5–10; 1 Peter 5: 6–11; Psalm 18:27–36; 34:1–4.
When you need guidance: Psalm 32:8; John 14:23–27.
When you need courage: Joshua 1:9; Exodus 14:23–27.
When someone does you wrong: Matthew 6:14, 15; Luke 23:33, 34.

POWER THOUGHT

Get acquainted with God's ways through God's Word.

◆ 9 ◆
The Referee Is for the Home Team

What would you think if you went to the gym for a game with another school and were told, "All of you know the rules, so we won't need a referee for this game. Each player will be responsible for calling his own fouls and other violations"?

Do you think it would work? Of course not. There would probably be a big fight in less than ten minutes. The players need the referee's help in enforcing the rules and keeping the action going.

And yet most of us don't like referees. It's kind of like Robert Frost's poem, "Something there is that doesn't like a wall. . . ." There's something about us that we don't like someone putting limits upon us, telling us what we can and cannot do. And that's part of what a referee does. He is the keeper of the limits. He blows the whistle when we exceed the agreed-upon rules. He says, "This is as a wall; you can go no further."

Yes, referees are people too. They get upset when mistreated . . . angry when taunted. Yet the good ones act as tough as a boot.

And I promise, in some games I've played in, the referee was my best friend. Without him, I would have been out cold on the floor.

The referee is there to keep order — not to hinder the game. And although I've gotten as upset as anybody with what I felt was a bad call, I still understood the importance of the referee's part in the game.

As Christians in the game of life, we have a spiritual referee in the person of the Holy Spirit. Like the basketball official, his purpose is to help, not to hinder, the progress of the game by reminding each player of the rules he already knows, explaining the things that might be confusing, and calling attention to mistakes.

The Holy Spirit does not make mistakes or wrong calls, and he is never partial to one player or team over another. You can trust him always to be right and always to be interested in your personal welfare. He is a merciful Referee. He doesn't give up on us after five fouls. He keeps blowing the whistle, explaining where we went wrong, and pointing us back to the right path.

As a player, I was taught never to argue with the referee — to accept his decisions without protest. And over the years I saw many other players — and coaches — find out the hard way that questioning the wisdom of the referee by opposing his calls was not wise.

To be a winner in life we need not only to know the rules but to be guided by the Holy Spirit in following them. He will lead you, teach you, guide you, reprove you, comfort you, dwell with you, and give you power and strength to play your best.

POWER THOUGHT

God's Referee, the Holy Spirit, is on your side!

◆ 10 ◆
Don't Foul Out

As a young ball player, I had fairly fast hands. But I got into the habit of hitting down on the ball when I was trying to take it away from an opponent. Sometimes I was successful, but more often than not I would foul.

When I got into college, Coach Abe Lemons saw my problem right away. One day he said to me, "Have you ever watched K. C. Jones, the great guard for the Boston Celtics? He always comes up on the ball. That makes it easier to get, and if you accidentally hit your opponent's hand it doesn't make as much noise. That lessens your chances of getting a foul."

I took the coach's advice and tried to change the way I played. It worked! I began to steal the ball more often and commit fewer fouls. It made me a better player.

Webster defines the word *foul* as any action which violates or is outside the accepted rules or limits of a contest or game.

In basketball, the player who commits a foul causes his team to be penalized. And after his fifth personal foul, he is removed from the game and not allowed to play anymore.

No matter how aggressive or skillful a player may be, if he commits fouls he will get caught and soon be out of the game. He will find, to his dismay, that the rules apply to everyone equally — that he is not above them or exempt from them.

The same is true in the game of life. Those who try to take shortcuts, to bend the rules, never get away with it for long. Sooner or later they foul out — of school, in marriage, in business, and in their Christian walk.

When you make a violation on the basketball court, the

referee blows the whistle. When you make a violation in your walk with Christ, the Holy Spirit calls "foul."

When you accept Christ, the Holy Spirit comes into your heart to live and to give you a super-sensitive conscience. Some of the things that may never have bothered you before, you will recognize as being outside the rules — foul. As a Christian, not only will you be concerned about your actions, but your thought life will become extremely important.

When you become a Christian you may have to change your style of play. You may have to work on some habits and your life style. But don't get discouraged. God wants to keep you in the game. He wants you to play... and to win.

Each time you hear the whistle of your conscience giving you a warning, simply change your direction, correct your behavior, and head toward the goal.

POWER THOUGHT

The same Holy Spirit that warns you of a foul is also your strength to find a new and better way.

Dahlgren Methodist Church
Dahlgren, Virginia 22448

◆ 11 ◆
If Your Temper Scores...
You Lose

You're in a hurry, and the combination lock won't open.
Your temper flares!

The coach gets on your case...and you see red!

You lose the ball on a scoring drive. *Temper!*

The referee calls a foul which you *know* you didn't
commit. And you lose your cool!

How you handle temper can make the difference in
winning or losing — in a game and in life as well.

Tempers have flared at many major sports events in
recent years. Because a moment of tension was not
handled properly, fights have occurred, injuries have
been suffered, and in some cases, near riots have
resulted which involved both players and fans.

You've probably read of multimillion-dollar lawsuits
being filed against some professional sports figures
because of their temper problems.

In some sports, acts of violence have almost become
trademarks. I heard of one man who said, "I went to a
fight the other night and a hockey game broke out!"

Failure to control your temper is always defeating —
to yourself and to those around you. Often a game is lost
because a player gets mad and either fouls out or makes
mistakes the opposing team can take advantage of.

Later on in life, temper may affect you in different
ways. The car won't start, and you'll be grouchy all day
long. You'll have a disagreement with your wife, and
people will stay out of your way for three days. Your job
may not be going right, sales might be down, and the
kids will get noisy at home. You explode into foot-

stomping fury. And everyone asks, "What's wrong with him?"

The Gospels tell of the betrayal of Jesus in the Garden of Gethsemane. When he saw the mob and their rough treatment of his Lord, Peter drew his sword and cut off a man's ear — I've always assumed he intended to do worse than that! But Jesus never lost control of the situation. He told Peter to put his sword away, and he healed the ear of the injured man.

You can win over temper. The secret of victory involves allowing Christ to live through you. Paul declared, "And the peace of God, which passeth all understanding, shall keep your hearts and minds through Christ Jesus" (Philippians 4:7).

POWER THOUGHT

"He that is soon angry dealeth foolishly" (Proverbs 14:17).

◆ 12 ◆
Tough It Out

Most athletes are familiar with the phrase, "Tape it up...tough it out." It means that you can't let pain stop you — you've got to keep going. One of the first lessons of practice and training is that you go on even when you think you can't. Playing with blisters, taped fingers, taped ankles is just part of the game. It's like one day in practice a boy yelled at another, "Hey, you fouled me!"

The coach walked over and said, jokingly, "Ah, it must not have been a foul — there's no blood!"

But it was no joke when one of Coach Abe Lemons' teams was playing out west and a player caught an elbow in the face and his tooth fell out. The referee did nothing. Coach Lemons grabbed the tooth and ran over to the scorers' table. "Some of the places where we play they call this a foul!" he shouted.

I remember how, during a game in Miami, Florida, I caught an elbow in the ribs. I doubled up with pain, and my chest felt like it had totally caved in.

After the game, on the way back to the hotel, one of my teammates noticed that I was still groaning. "When does it hurt, Larry?"

"Every time I take a breath," I replied.

"That's simple," he said comfortingly. "Just stop breathing."

I ended up having to wear a brace, and for months I had tremendous chest pain when I exerted myself. But I kept going. I could hear the words of the coach in my ears, "You can make it! Tough it out!"

Many times off the basketball court it's hard to keep going. It would be much easier to say, "I quit."

In Bible days, one of the punishments for murder was

"tribulation." The offender would be stretched out on the ground and a large slab of stone would be laid on top of him. Then several men would get on the rock and jump up and down, literally pressing the life out of the condemned man. That is the meaning of tribulation: "to be pressed out."

You may feel that life has pressed you out. Perhaps you've ached as your parents went through a divorce. Or you may have experienced racial prejudice, or the cruel limitations of a physical handicap. Your life may have been scarred mentally and emotionally, and you know all about tribulation.

Jesus has something to say to you. No, he doesn't promise to take away all pain or tears. He simply says, "You're going to make it. I've been right where you are. I've walked down that path ahead of you. And there's nothing there that together we can't overcome."

With Christ you can overcome. Even in the midst of being pressed out, hurting, even crying — you can know that you're going to make it. Toughing it out pays off. Jesus Christ has overcome the world. He has overcome your situation. And you are on his team.

POWER THOUGHT

"I can do all things through Christ which strengtheneth me" (Philippians 4:13).

◆ 13 ◆
Today's Practice Is Tomorrow's Game

Basketball is a game of seconds!

A player cannot stay in the lane for more than three seconds at his end of the court.

A team has ten seconds to get the ball across the mid-court line when it takes possession.

If a defensive player stays within three feet of an offensive player for five seconds or more while they are between the mid-court line and the top of the circle, it's a jump ball. When you're in the heat of a game it's easy to forget — to delay those few precious seconds that make the difference in a referee's whistle or a successful play. Those crucial seconds could well make the difference between winning or losing the game.

The only way to be confident in these tight spots in game situations is to discipline yourself on the right steps to take while you're practicing. If you never allow yourself to violate the three-second rule during practice, you won't be as likely to do it during a game. The same holds for bringing the ball down court . . . or defensing a player.

And if you have the attitude that you won't do in practice what you don't want to do in play, you won't have to unlearn bad habits. Remember that you are really playing when you are practicing. What you do on the practice court carries over into the game. As my coach said so many times, "You will never play better than you practice." So practice the tight spots, and at game time you'll play them well.

So it is in life. Every day is practice day. Every good

deed done becomes a habit. Every time of prayer, meditation, Bible study builds resources for the day when you will need that extra reserve. The crucial difference will come at the moment of temptation and trial.

It's too easy to think of the heroes of faith and not realize the "practice time" they put in. One of my favorite sections of Scripture is Hebrews 11. Some call it the "Roll Call of Faith." It included Noah, Abraham, Moses, Gideon, David, and many more of whom the writer said,

They were stoned, they were sawn asunder, were tempted, were slain with the sword: they wandered about in sheepskins and goatskins; being destitute, afflicted, tormented. . . they wandered in deserts, and in mountains, and in dens and caves of the earth.

That's no easy sainthood. . . no simple step to being a great Christian. It takes practice time: practicing the faith, living the reality of Christ within, a reality which enables us to live better, shoot higher, and realize more than we ever thought possible.

POWER THOUGHT

Bad habits never learned, never have to be unlearned.

◆ 14 ◆
Playing One Game at a Time

One of the worst things that can happen to a good team, is when they forget to concentrate on the team they're playing now. Instead, they begin to think about the big game right after this one. As a consequence, what should have been an easy game — almost a pushover — is lost and they're greatly embarrassed. They were caught looking past their opponent. . .failing to play one game at a time. It happens a lot, not only in basketball but in life as well. Failure to concentrate on this moment, on this time in life.

I'm sure you've wanted at times to think about other things. . .not to worry about the problems you're facing today. . .to postpone dealing with them so that you can think about the promise of fun tomorrow. But those problems of today can really louse up tomorrow.

As a young man, I was interested in the present, but I was also concerned about where I would be in ten years — if I would be happy and successful. I wondered what I would be doing in a career, what kind of car I would drive, to whom I would be married, how many children we would have — all the same things you've probably wondered about.

In the process of worrying about ten years from now I could have failed to concentrate on the moment. . .on the things that were important today.

This moment is the most important one in our lives. That means concentrating on what's important now, rather than putting it off until later. In order to be where God wants you to be ten years from now, you have to do God's will *today*. Jesus said, "Seek ye first the kingdom of

God, and his righteousness; and all these things shall be added unto you" (Matthew 6:33).

Living for Christ happens one day at a time. And after you begin to approach it that way, here are some key thoughts to help you.

1. *Know that you're number one in God's eyes.* The One who watches the fall of the sparrow and knows the hairs on your head is also very concerned about you and your life. Everything you do, every problem you face is on his agenda.

2. *Know that he will be with you in every step you take.* None of us is always able to know the best step. It's like in basketball: sometimes we zig when we should have zagged. But God's not an angry tyrant ready to throw us out. Rather, he's suffering when we suffer, he's rejoicing when we rejoice, and he's a part of all we do.

3. *Don't try to do everything at once.* A winning season is important to players, coaches, and fans. But the way a winning season is realized is by winning games one at a time. No one can ever have a winning season by playing the season all at once. A winner does it by winning games one at a time. So it is in life. Deal with each of your problems one step at a time. Work on improving your life daily. Don't postpone the inevitable hard decision but work a little bit on it right now.

4. *Don't give up when you fail.* No one wins all the time. The best players, coaches, and teams lose at one time or another. Even Jesus lost at times. The disciples lost. God has lost. And you're going to lose. But God never has given up on his players. Jesus kept on loving even when it cost him his life. The disciples hung in there and eventually experienced the victory that life in Christ can bring.

5. *Remember, Christian, there's always a tomorrow.* We can't recall all our mistakes. Some games are lost and there's nothing we can do about it. But we will have other opportunities. . .other chances to be what we want to be. God is the God of second chances. You have that same chance too.

"Trust in the Lord with all thine heart; and lean not unto thine own understanding. In all thy ways acknowledge him, and he shall direct thy paths" (Proverbs 3:5, 6).

◆ 15 ◆
Butterflies

The last practice before the game is over. You go to the showers and clean up, then try to get some rest. And here come the butterflies!

Lying in bed looking up at the ceiling, you find yourself trying to play the coming game in your mind. Will the other team be as good as everybody says? Will your man overpower you and make you look bad? Will you remember the new plays? Before you know it, your stomach has become the playground for the flitting, fluttering antics of the butterflies of anxiety and tension.

Almost every athlete has had to learn to deal with pre-game butterflies. In fact, butterflies bother speakers, singers, actors — all kinds of performers who must face some challenge at an appointed time.

Butterflies breed in other places besides gyms, playing fields, or performance stages. They seem to fly into your life on many occasions — usually just at the wrong time.

Perhaps you have a big decision to make — one that can have important consequences for the rest of your life. You consider the facts, sift through the information you have, and tentatively make up your mind. But you aren't absolutely sure about it. And here come the butterflies of fear and worry.

Maybe you're in love and have decided to get married. You set the date. Then comes a misunderstanding you didn't expect. And the butterfly of uncertainty flutters by.

You make plans for the future — career, home, education. But as you begin working your plans, there is an accident, unforeseen trouble, a death in the family. And the butterfly of the unexpected casts a shadow that seems to shut off the sun.

What you need is a "butterfly net" that will help you catch and control those troubling pests that eat away at your confidence and peace of mind. Psalm 34 seems to have been made to order for this purpose.

The entire chapter is good, but verse one gives you the key. David said, "I will bless the Lord at *all* times." As you keep your mind on the Lord, butterflies are screened out.

What if they're already in? Verse 4 promises that God will deliver you from all butterflies — especially fears. And down in verse 19 David warns that you will have to contend with many butterflies, but the Lord will give you victory over each one.

Whenever you feel that old uneasiness in your stomach and hear the rustle of butterfly wings, go back to Psalm 34 for reassurance and confidence. Remind yourself, as David must have, that the God who gave him victory over a bear, a lion, and a giant certainly wouldn't let him be defeated by a butterfly.

POWER THOUGHT

"I know whom I have believed, and am persuaded that he is able to keep that which I have committed unto him . . ." (2 Timothy 1:12).

◆ 16 ◆
The Crowd Is for You

Observers of sporting events over the years have noticed that the home team has the crowd advantage. Obviously, most of the fans attending a game will be for the local team.

The physical presence of friendly fans, with their cheers and emotional support, has a tremendous positive effect on an athletic team. Hearing the shouts of support from the stands is a great encouragement to the individual players.

One year Oklahoma City University's basketball team was playing Miami University, at Miami. OCU had never beaten them on their own court. And by half time, they were behind by twelve points.

Then something tremendous and exciting happened. The OCU fans who made the trip began to come alive and really cheer for their team. They were led by Dr. Joe Blinco, who had been a Billy Graham associate evangelist. His daughter was an OCU student and so he had gone with her to the game.

When the second half started, he yelled and cheered so enthusiastically that the mood of the whole crowd changed. Soon all the OCU fans were on their feet, urging their team on. The home crowd couldn't figure out what was happening. The OCU team got fired up. They played over their heads — better than they had ever played. They caught up with Miami and the game ended with a score of 105-105.

The OCU fans went wild and cheered even louder. The whole atmosphere was charged with excitement. Sure enough, OCU won the game in overtime, 118-113.

The writer of Hebrews teaches that the Christian crowd

is to band together and support each other in the game of life. He said, "Let us consider one another to provoke unto love and to good works: Not forsaking the assembling of ourselves together . . . but exhorting one another" (10:24, 25).

The fellowship of Christian believers is vital. Being part of the pep squad helps keep us encouraged in the faith.

After spending the entire eleventh chapter of his letter on a roll call of the heroes of faith, the author of Hebrews assures us that these fellow team members are watching us from heaven, cheering us on. He could almost have been describing the crowd at the Olympic games in Rome as they cheered their favorites on to victory.

"Wherefore seeing we also are compassed about with so great a cloud of witnesses, let us lay aside every weight, and the sin which doth so easily beset us, and let us run with patience the race that is set before us" (12:1).

POWER THOUGHT

As a runner in the race that ends in heaven, you have the home crowd advantage.

Get off the Bench

As far as I know, Abraham Lincoln never played
basketball. But he said something about the game of life
that many coaches try to teach their players.

Lincoln said, "I will prepare, and when my time
comes, I will be ready!"

Young players sometimes find it difficult to give 100
percent in every practice when they know they aren't on
the starting team — the first five. They sometimes
develop the attitude that says, "What's the use? I won't
get to play in the game anyway. If I put out, I only make
the starters better because they have to work harder to
keep their position."

But the second five players are tremendously
important to any team. They provide the depth a team
must have to be a championship contender. As
substitutes, they are in a position to gain valuable
experience. They keep the first team on its toes. And they
are ready to step in at a moment's notice to give another
player a rest, or to take his place if he gets hurt.

Often you will hear a sports analyst say, "The game
may well be decided by which team has the best bench."
He is saying that the starting teams are about equal and
that the quality of the second team — or the
substitutes — could make the difference.

Moses was the leader of the children of Israel when
they left Egypt and made their way across the wilderness
toward the Promised Land. But it was Joshua, the second
teamer, who led the people into Canaan. After Moses
grew old and died, Joshua moved up and became the
leader. Why? Because he had spent more than forty
years as the second man, in training to be number one.
When his time came, he was ready.

God said to Joshua, "As I was with Moses, so I will be with thee: I will not fail thee, nor forsake thee" (Joshua 1:5).

I'm sure there were times during his forty years on the bench when Joshua wondered if it was worth it to keep giving his best day after day. He may have felt that God wasn't even noticing his efforts. It probably was hard to see the reward for all the aches and sweat and dust. But he kept on preparing. And his time did come.

God has not forgotten you, either. He has placed you in a position to help the team and be a part of the kingdom of God. The role you play now may be designed to prepare you for a greater ministry . . . in God's own time.

One thing you can count on: you will be on the squad that marches into the Promised Land!

POWER THOUGHT

Now is the time to prepare for God's service so that when his time for you comes, you will be ready.

◆ 18 ◆
Give It All
You've Got

Every successful basketball team spends a great deal of its practice — and playing time — working on defense. There are some coaches who feel that defense is the most important part of the game.

Others are offense minded. They love to see their team in their opponent's court. They know that is the way to score. . . and to win.

But the great teams that I've watched do a combination of both. They can put on a full court press that's like glue. And if they're big around the boards, as soon as they snag a rebound it's hurled down the court to a breaking guard. It's hustle, run and gun, dee-fense. And it's fun to watch.

Yet some teams may have just as good a record without a great offensive and defensive capability. And a lot of times it has to do with good coaching. The coach knows what his players can do and what they can't do. Consequently, he adjusts the team's style of play to its capabilities as well as its limitations.

And that's a Christian idea too. Jesus told the story about the man who distributed different amounts of money to three of his employees. They were supposed to put the money to work for him. Two of them did so, but one employee simply hid his and did nothing with it. He was strongly reprimanded.

We can't all be seven feet tall, faster than anyone else, or great outside shooters. But we can hustle as hard as anyone else. We can practice as much as anyone else, and we can work at improving as much as anyone else.

And that's what playing a sport in school is all about anyway.

It's the same in our Christian life. There are others who may be able to speak better, witness more effectively, and understand the Bible more clearly. But their ability is not our concern. Our task is using our talents and our capabilities to their fullest. And that means finding ways that we can be effective Christians. Our task may be different from that of our best friend. But the important thing is that we are faithful in fulfilling our own responsibilities.

POWER THOUGHT

Lord, help me to use what I have.

◆ 19 ◆
Practicing to Win

Basketball can get into your blood. Once you've gotten used to the feel of the hardwood as you dribble down court, it's hard to give it up. It's a great feeling to go in for a layup or bounce a pass inside to your forward for two quick ones. The swish through the net, driving, faking. . . it's all part of a great game.

But there's one essential part of basketball that's no fun at all and that's hard practice. . . I mean the kind in which you run up and down the court and do the same play over and over. After awhile you get to thinking practice and basketball are two different things. The latter is fun; the other is murder.

But winning at basketball takes both. When basketball is no longer fun, you don't play as well. And when you don't practice you don't win.

Indiana's great basketball coach, Bobby Knight, once said, "Everyone wants to be a winner, but few are willing to do the practicing necessary to win."

Another way of putting that is that most of us want to be on a winning team, but not all of us are willing to do the hard work necessary before that can happen.

Strangely enough, the Christian life is a lot like that. Too many times it's portrayed as a simple thing you do once and forget about. But it goes far beyond that. Someone once said, "The easiest thing in the world is accepting Christ; but it takes a lifetime to understand what that means."

That's another way of saying that living for Christ takes heads-up play, dedication, and hard work. It takes working at understanding what it means to be a Christlike person in today's very unchristlike world.

And nothing is more important to that than regular church attendance, private Bible study and prayer, and serious attempts with others to understand how to live out one's faith in today's world.

POWER THOUGHT

Lord, help me to practice living my faith.

◆ 20 ◆
When You're Not Hitting

Several years ago, Ken Tricky, when he was head coach
at Oral Roberts University, talked about his superstar
player, All-American Richard Fuqua, who had led the
nation in scoring. He said, "What makes Richard a
superstar is that he's not just a one-dimensional player.
Sure, he's a great shooter, but when he's not hitting his
shot, he doesn't let that ruin the rest of his game. He still
hustles on defense, keeps his passing sharp, and doesn't
let up."

That's hard to do. When one part of your game goes
bad, it's tough not to let it affect the rest.

I've seen it happen a lot. A player's shots don't fall in,
so he slows down on everything else. He doesn't push
quite as hard to get down the court to his position, and
consequently misses the pass that he should have had.
He gets angry and lets fly with a too-quick shot that
misses the basket altogether. He fails to make anything
happen on defense. He's letting one part of his game
cause a total defeat.

So it is in life. When one bad thing happens, if we
don't watch out, soon it will affect everything else we're
doing. We'll be down on everything and everybody,
unwilling to put out that extra effort that really makes the
difference in life.

It can happen to anybody... even preachers. There
have been times in our "Feed the Children" program that
I've had food to feed the starving ready for shipment...
and then had to wait weeks for some bureaucratic red
tape to unravel. Meanwhile, people — especially little
children — were dying from lack of food. When that
happens I get angry, upset, and frustrated. And if I don't

watch, that feeling will creep over into my other work and relationships. From hard experience I've had to learn that I can only do my best and then leave everything in the hands of the Lord and proceed with the other tasks he has for me.

Even though sometimes we don't feel like trying, and our attitude has gone down the tube. . .that may be the time to realize, "Hey! One part isn't the whole. There are other things I can do well. I'll concentrate on them!"

POWER THOUGHT

"Be instant in season and out of season" (2 Timothy 4:2).

◆ 21 ◆
Rebound! Rebound!

My college basketball team was known for "runnin' and gunnin'." And it was great as long as we were hitting. We often had three players score twenty or more points in the same game.

But if we were not hitting, it was Trouble City. We hadn't worked nearly so hard at getting the rebounds, the garbage shots. And it hurt us as a result. Without someone to rebound the misses, it can be a long night.

The same is true in the Christian life. You will experience victory and defeat. You will shoot . . . you will attempt; sometimes you will miss . . . you will fail. But when a ball player shoots and misses, he doesn't quit. He rebounds and shoots again. And that's exactly what you have to do as a Christian.

During my basketball days I discovered some good rebound verses in my Bible, and they have continued to help me. I think they'll help you too.

"I can do all things through Christ which strengtheneth me" (Philippians 4:13). "Greater is he that is in you, than he that is in the world" (1 John 4:4).

It's no disgrace to fail — to miss the mark — but it is a disgrace not to get up and try again. Some of the Bible's greatest heroes of faith had to learn how to face failure before they were able to succeed — men like Moses, Jacob, David, Jonah, Peter . . . and many others.

When you read about these saints, you may have a tendency to glorify them. But the truth is that they made mistakes, had weaknesses, and missed the mark just as all of us do. We all have to deal with failure at some point in our lives. The important thing is not to give up.

This was true of the first followers of Jesus. They were given the name "Christian," which means *little Christ*, first in the city of Antioch because the people saw Christ's likeness in them. Yet the Bible records their faults along with their spiritual strengths. Their perfection was measured in terms of the perfection of Christ, who lived in them, and their relationship to him. They made mistakes, but *they never quit trying.*

So if you are struggling with your misses, maybe you need to rebound and ask Christ to help you. A missed shot doesn't mean the game is over. REBOUND!

POWER THOUGHT

When you miss. . .rebound!

◆ 22 ◆
Pass It On

"Pass the ball! Pass the ball!"

Just about every player in the gym hears that phrase hundreds of times during the season. Coaches yell it from the sidelines. Teammates shout it from their position on the court. Passing the ball is good offensive strategy. Usually if the ball is moved quickly around the floor someone will get a good open shot.

In basketball, the person who passes the ball to someone else for a shot that scores is given credit for an assist. Players with good assist records are regarded just as highly as good shooters.

I used to enjoy watching Wesley Unseld of the Washington Bullets move the ball. The moment he rebounded on the defensive boards he passed to a teammate to get the ball down the floor. Many times his action led to a quick basket for his team.

After a person comes into a vital relationship with Christ, he is immediately faced with the challenge to pass on his new faith. To become a productive member of Christ's team, the new believer should share the gospel of Jesus Christ with someone else.

In other words, you simply give what you've got. You don't have to be a scholar or theologian to be an effective witness. All you have to do is tell what God has done for you. So you are qualified to be a witness for the Lord: a passer — an assister. Are you passing on your faith to those about you who need to hear about Christ?

An alert basketball player passes the ball to the first open teammate he sees. And he does it quickly, before the opportunity is blocked. Is there someone near you who is open to the gospel? Then don't put off going to that person as soon as you can. You might never have the opportunity again. Don't hide your faith — share it. Don't keep it — give it away.

Perhaps you know someone you could share with today. So get going. Time is running out. Pass it on! Pass it on! Remember the mandate from our Lord: "Go ye into all the world and preach the gospel to every creature" (Mark 16:15).

POWER THOUGHT

To be a good team player for Christ, simply share what has happened in your own life. Give what you've got; tell what you know. "Freely ye have received, freely give" (Matthew 10:8).

◆ 23 ◆
Blocked Shot Syndrome

I am just six feet tall. Most basketball players are much taller. My roommate in college was six feet, ten inches tall. So as a young ball player I learned to shoot quickly, or one of the taller players would not only block the shot but cram the ball back into my face!

After having a few shots blocked by taller or more skillful players, it is easy to develop what coaches call the "blocked shot syndrome." You feel it when you get close to the goal, almost in position to shoot. It causes you to be jittery, jumpy, reluctant to take a shot. Something inside you cringes at the thought of the shot being blocked and crammed back at you. Knowing this, some coaches have encouraged their leapers and big men to try blocking shots early in the game to create that uncertainty in the opposition.

Just one blocked shot can affect a player for weeks, as well as changing the tone of a whole ball game. If an individual can't shake off the syndrome, his effectiveness as a player can be totally destroyed.

There is a form of the "blocked shot syndrome" that can affect you in the game of life. It's not at all unusual for things not to go as you had planned. You may make the wrong decision, or simply try and fail. You suggest a solution for a problem and someone else has a better idea. Blocked shot!

But you must not let a temporary setback ruin your whole game. Get back in position, go for the ball, and shoot again.

Try another angle, move in from another direction, come back the same way you did before — but don't quit. Keep trying. You may get blocked six times, but the seventh shot will get through and score!

Have you ever considered the story of Joseph in the Bible? It is one of the most amazing accounts of persistence and unwavering faith you'll ever read.

First, Joseph's jealous brothers decided to do him in and dumped him in a deep pit to die. Then they sold him to some traders who offered him for sale to an Egyptian named Potiphar. Then Potiphar's wife lied and accused him of assaulting her — and he ended up in prison.

Three blocked shots! But Joseph didn't let them get him down. He refused to be defeated by the blocked shot syndrome. He stayed true to God. . . and kept his faith.

And it paid off. From the depths of the dungeon, Joseph ended up in Pharaoh's palace. From there he was able to save an entire nation — and his own people — during a time of severe famine.

What if Joseph had quit in despair? But he didn't, and he ended up on the winning team.

You can overcome the blocked shot syndrome in your life. It means you have to go right back to the same place where you were defeated before. It means you have to keep on trying. It means you have to risk being blocked again. But you can win if you keep on trying.

POWER THOUGHT

In basketball or the game of life, persistence pays off. Winners are those who will not be defeated.

◆ 24 ◆
Assist and Screen

Good basketball involves teamwork. While individual skill and effort are important, the teams that win are made up of players who have learned how to work together.

Two of the most frequent team plays are the "assist" and the "screen." An assist is when a player throws the ball to a teammate and the pass leads directly to a goal. A screen is when one player stands in the way of a defensive player so his teammate can drive around for a possible goal.

One of the first lessons young players have to learn is that basketball is not a game for the Lone Ranger — it must be played by a team.

Nor is the Christian life to be lived in solitude. As Christians, we need each other. Think about how you became a Christian. Chances are there were a number of people involved in influencing you and bringing you to Christ. You probably were touched spiritually by friends, parents, coaches, pastors, youth workers, grandparents, evangelists, and others. There were many whose fingerprints of love and concern were placed on you.

In 1 Corinthians 3, Paul suggests that this is just the way God intended for his work to be done. He says we are laborers together with God, that one plants a seed, another waters it. . . and God gives the harvest.

Someone once speculated that the average individual may receive twenty witnesses about the Lord before he makes a decision to accept Christ. If that is true, for every person who gives the twentieth witness and helps lead a soul to Christ, there are nineteen others who shared the gospel but saw no immediate results. Are you willing to be witness number nineteen? Or number eight, or twelve, or two?

God calls some to gather in the harvest of souls. But if there is to be a harvest, there must also be those who plant the seeds of the gospel, and those who water them. No function on God's team is unimportant.

I am an evangelist. During our area-wide crusades we often see hundreds of people make decisions for Christ. Nothing excites me more. But I am well aware that what is accomplished is a team effort.

First of all, you see, there are the people in the community who are praying for a movement of God's Spirit in their area. Laymen, Sunday school teachers, pastors, and others all prepare the ground. Then one of my team goes in and helps set up some fourteen committees to begin making preparations for the coming meeting. Another staff member meets with counselors and teaches them how to lead people to Christ. Still another teammate spends the entire week of the crusade visiting with new converts and teaching a class each day on "How to Share Your Faith." Special musicians travel with me to provide special music, and I preach a gospel message each night.

To be successful, our crusades must have the best efforts of all the people working together. No one individual or group could do it alone.

When a person comes to Christ, look at how many people have reached out to touch him. It could be literally hundreds.

Are you putting your fingerprints on lost people for the cause of Christ? Are you assisting others to find Jesus? Keep on doing your best. And remember what a very wise missionary once said: "There is no limit to what you can help accomplish for the kingdom of God if you don't care who gets the credit."

POWER THOUGHT

"And let us not be weary in well doing: for in due season we shall reap, if we faint not" (Galatians 6:9).

◆ 25 ◆
Hot Dog

You can spot a "hot dog" a mile away. They are the guys who must be seen. Their pictures must be in the paper. Everyone must know how great they are. They seek out everybody's praise. They must be number one. They are the hot dogs.

During an important game toward the end of the season, one of the "bench warmers" kept tugging at the coach's sleeve and asking to be put in. The coach was surprised. The boy had never been an outstanding player and had never pushed himself before. But he was insistent that the coach give him a chance in this particular game.

Finally the coach gave in and sent the boy out on the court. To everybody's amazement, the young man played like a house on fire. He was everywhere, assisting, screening, shooting, scoring, and shouting encouragement to the rest of the team. In fact, he scored as many points in that one game as he had the rest of the season combined.

After the game was over, the coach went to the boy to ask what had happened to him — why there had been such a drastic change in his playing. The boy said quietly, "Coach, my dad passed away last week. He was blind and never got to see me play. I knew that in heaven he would be able to see, and I thought he would be watching me today for the first time. So I played this game for him!"

There's no place for hot dogs in basketball or the Christian life. In his letter to the church at Corinth, Paul explained that we are all part of the body of Christ. For the body to function properly each member must do its part. One member is not more important than the others. (See 1 Corinthians 12.)

Whatever we do should be done to glorify God and not to focus attention on ourself. If we are asked to sing or give our testimony, we can do it to the glory of God. If we are asked to clean off tables, we should do that for the glory of God. As the apostle said, "Whether therefore ye eat, or drink, or whatsoever ye do, do all to the glory of God" (1 Corinthians 10:31).

That's the attitude we should have as Christians. Our aim should be to play, not for our glory, but for the glory of God. And we should play every game for him.

POWER THOUGHT

Do your best for the glory of God. "And thy Father, which seeth in secret, shall reward thee openly" (Matthew 6:18).

◆ 26 ◆
The Jealous Bug

A boy makes a great pass to his buddy, who hits the basket and wins the game! The buddy's picture goes in the paper along with a score of the game winning shot . . . and there is not a word about the pass.

A football lineman makes a great block and the halfback slips through a hole for a touchdown. The sports page headlines talk about the skill of the running back . . . and nothing at all about the lineman.

One of the first things you have to learn in sports and in the game of life is that life is not always fair. There is not equal recognition for equal effort, equal pay for equal work, equal opportunity for equal preparedness. Things just don't always work out the way you think they should. This is not negative thinking. It is simply exposing the principles of sheltered idealism to the cold, hard light of everyday reality.

All through life you will probably not get as much credit as you think you should have for what you are, what you know, or what you do. So what do you do about it? Do you just laugh and go on? Get mad and sulk? Let up and stop doing your job?

When the jealous bug bites an athlete, the poison that spreads through his system can not only ruin him but also infect the whole team. When one person starts worrying about personal recognition, he begins to put the welfare of the team second and his own interests first. And the harmony and comradeship of the team can be painfully disrupted when one person is jealous over the praise another team member receives.

I have appreciated seeing some of the athletes, who were singled out to receive special achievement awards in recent years, stand and give public testimony to the help they received from others on the team. One Heisman trophy winner for football said flatly, "This should be a team award because I wouldn't be here without the work the other guys did to make me look good."

The jealous bug can be just as dangerous to a family, a church, or a business. One person ends up in the limelight and the others feel left out. If they aren't careful, they will begin to resent the "star" instead of rejoicing with him and being proud of the honor the accomplishment brings to the entire group.

Jesus said, "Greater love hath no man than this, that a man lay down his life for his friends." (See John 15:13.)

A girl sings a solo with a voice so clear and pure it seems the angels even stop to listen. When the song is ended, everybody raves about how beautifully she sang. No one remembers the accompanist, or the voice teacher, or the parents who sacrificed to pay for her voice lessons. But love fills their hearts as they watch her take her bows. Their great love finds fulfillment in her success.

When you find yourself in an exposed position and you feel the first prick of the jealous bug's bite, stamp on the demonic insect and kill it before it destroys you. Then let love bathe the wound where it bit you. You will be healed.

POWER THOUGHT

"Be kindly affectioned one to another with brotherly love; in honour preferring one another" (Romans 12:10).

◆ 27 ◆
Walking with the Ball

You can dribble the ball, pass it, shoot it. . . but you can't walk with the ball or carry it. It's a violation of the rules, and getting caught results in the other team getting the ball. Walking with the ball is a no-no!

Sometimes a player is called for walking with the ball because he gets his body going faster than the ball. Other times he simply gets careless, or loses his pace or rhythm. Before he knows it, he has taken an extra step — and the whistle blows!

In the game of life, walking and carrying your troubles is a no-no! The Bible says over and over that you are to give your troubles to the Lord and not try to bear them by yourself. Mark these spiritual rules in your Bible and remind yourself of them often:

Psalm 55:22: "Cast thy burden upon the Lord, and he shall sustain thee."
1 Peter 5:7: "Casting all your care upon him; for he careth for you."
Philippians 4:6: "Be careful for nothing; but in every thing by prayer and supplication with thanksgiving let your requests be made known unto God."

At times your life may get to moving so fast that you find yourself juggling a whole pack full of troubles instead of leaving them with the Lord. Or so many troubles come at once that you forget to carry them to God in prayer. And then the whistle blows, the play is dead, and the game is stopped for you until you begin handling the "ball" properly again.

In many sports, athletes train and practice for

competition with extra weight fastened to their bodies. Perhaps you've noticed a baseball player swinging three or four bats before he goes into the batter's box. But he does not carry the extra weight with him. He carries only his regular bat, which feels light and easy to handle by comparison to the load he has been carrying.

In the early days of olympic competition centuries ago, runners would wear heavy clothes or wear metal chains around their neck until time for the race. It is this practice that the writer of Hebrews referred to when he said, "Let us lay aside every weight, and the sin which doth so easily beset us, and let us run with patience the race that is set before us" (Hebrews 12:1).

So let me remind you that the game has started, the race is underway. It's time to lay aside the weights that hold you back. . .get rid of the extra weights and burdens. Stop walking with the ball.

The best advice I can give you is found in the words of an old, old song of the church:

What a friend we have in Jesus,
All our sins and griefs to bear,
What a privilege to carry
Everything to God in prayer.
Oh, what peace we often forfeit,
Oh, what needless pain we bear,
All because we do not carry
Everything to God in prayer.

POWER THOUGHT

"Fear thou not; for I am with thee: be not dismayed; for I am thy God: I will strengthen thee; yea, I will help thee; yea, I will uphold thee with the right hand of my righteousness" (Isaiah 41:10).

◆ 28 ◆
Out of Bounds

The basketball court has certain well-marked boundary lines, and all the action of the game is supposed to take place inside that area.

Games have actually been lost because someone stepped out of bounds, and what would have been the winning basket didn't count. In one game I rushed toward the sideline so fast trying to keep the ball in bounds that I was forced to hurdle the sportswriters' table.

The game of life takes that kind of concern, too. Many young people I see are trying to convince themselves that drugs, booze, premarital sex, and other vices are okay. Deep down in their hearts they know those things are out of bounds. And if they submit to them they'll end up being thrown out of the game. . . permanently.

The truth is that much of the trouble and many of the penalties we suffer in life come from trying to play out of bounds. Instead of keeping our eyes on the right goal and moving in that direction, we're tempted to slip over the line and bend the rules just a little. If we do, it eventually will catch up with us.

All of us know of people who stepped out of bounds, who came to a crossing in the road and then took the wrong turn. . . who never realized the great potential that was there. There are plenty of examples in basketball.

One of the worst revolved around one of the most sought-after "big men" in America. He was 7'1" when he finished high school. And yet he was agile and smooth with a great hook. Unfortunately, he failed to meet the two criteria for admission to college on scholarship: either having graduated in the top half of his class, or scoring high enough on the SAT.

But this young man was unwilling to wait the compulsory one year to prove himself in the classroom. Instead he agreed to step out of bounds. And as any good athlete knows, there are plenty of people around who seem to thrive on breaking the rules, and encouraging young athletes to do the same. For him it started with his principal, who agreed to change his transcript, to show that he had indeed finished in the top half of his class.

For a while it looked like he would get by with it. He was outstanding as a freshman and sophomore. His team had moved into the top twenty, and it was destined for great things.

But something had happened inside. His attitude worsened. He wanted more. . .his school agreed. . . followed by more out-of-bounds play. Finally, he transferred to another college. . .also willing to play out of bounds. But it didn't help. He quit school in his senior year.

He tried the pros. Eventually, newspapers carried stories about his being in a gun fight. Later, a brief article mentioned he was playing in Italy. Now he's never heard of. It all started with one instance of stepping out of bounds.

The winning game is played in bounds, by the rules. To be a winner, we must observe God's commandments and learn the playing court so we know the boundaries of the Christian life. Then, by keeping our eyes on Christ, and following in his footsteps, we will always know where we are. . .and be able to avoid stepping out of bounds.

POWER THOUGHT

"Be not deceived; God is not mocked: for whatsoever a man soweth, that shall he also reap" (Galatians 6:7).

◆ 29 ◆
I Forgot the Play

"What happened out there?" demands the coach during a hastily called time-out.

And a crestfallen player hangs his head and mumbles, "I forgot the play."

Every athlete at one time or another has witnessed a scene such as this. And if he has played for any length of time, he probably remembers when he was in that embarrassing position.

All through life you are likely to be involved in situations in which somebody forgets the play. It is disappointing to be working hard for victory and have the team break down because someone is not where he is supposed to be, because of a forgotten play. It's easy to get upset with the offending team member.

Jesus said, "And when ye stand praying, forgive, if ye have ought against any: that your Father also which is in heaven may forgive you your trespasses" (Mark 11:25). He might have said, "Forgive when a team member forgets the play; then your heavenly Father will forgive you when you forget the play."

The game of life must have forgiveness as the alternate game plan. It is impossible for a team to function in an atmosphere of bitterness, resentment, and unforgiveness. That grates like sand in the machinery of life.

In high school, we had a team member who would get upset with the rest of the team if mistakes were made. He would go into the locker room at half time and sit with his back to everybody else, staring moodily into the corner. His body language just screamed, "We're behind because of you and your mistakes. You're causing me to lose!"

The coach spent a lot of time working on that young man's attitude. He had to learn to forgive and be a part of the team, errors or no errors, win or lose.

You will be on a lot of teams in life: your family, your company, your church. And there will be plenty of times when someone forgets the play and causes a mixup. The mistake might even put you behind in the game. And you may as well learn the lesson of forgiveness now.

Learning the art of forgiveness will be much more valuable to you than shooting, screening, or rebounding. All through life you will be forgiving — employers, employees, friends, children, wife, husband, family, or neighbors. Time and again the game plan will break down because someone forgot. And you have the choice of quitting the team. . .or forgiving and helping everybody get back into the game.

You may lose a ball game because someone forgot the play. But you will win in the game of life if you learn to forgive, regardless of the situation.

POWER THOUGHT

Peter asked Jesus how many times he should forgive his brother — seven times? And Jesus said, "Until seventy times seven" — which means, as often as he needs it! How many more times will God forgive you?

◆ 30 ◆
Expected Trouble...
Unexpected Trouble

There are two kinds of trouble a team can encounter in a ball game...the expected and the unexpected. Here's what I mean:

Most of the time your team knows about what to expect from its opponents. And your coaches usually have a good idea of your opponents and the strength and weakness of each of their players. Even if you've never played them before, someone will have scouted them and predicted what they will do. So before the game ever begins you know what to expect and how to plan your offense and defense.

Sometimes, though, you come up against a team you've never played or watched before. Or at the beginning of a new season, your opponent fields some players you know nothing about. They may even have developed some new plays that really catch you off guard. When any of this happens, you're suddenly facing unexpected trouble. How you handle it can be the difference between winning and losing.

And the same thing applies off the court. We are constantly confronted with different kinds of problems and concerns...many of them expected. For example, finding the right job, the right person to marry, making enough money to have a place to live, taking care of a family, dealing with temptation, doubt, and fear. Even when you expect them, there are tough problems we all eventually have to face.

But at times unexpected problems threaten to overwhelm us. They slip in from our blind side, or simply strike with such force and fury that we are caught off guard. Death, divorce, disappointment, business loss, natural disaster, or some other personal tragedy strikes. How do you withstand unexpected trouble?

I'm asked that question time and again. It's never easy. For example, some time ago I was asked to speak to a group of tornado victims. They had been right in the path of an unexpected storm which had destroyed everything they had. Hardly any of them had experienced a tornado before. Many of them had lost their neighbors, friends, and loved ones. . . and escaped themselves with only the clothes they had on their backs.

What do you say to such a group?

The Lord gave me a Bible text to share with them. It is good advice for all of us. The psalmist wrote: "He shall not be afraid of evil tidings: his heart is fixed, trusting in the Lord" (Psalm 112:7).

This is the only way to prepare for unexpected trouble. Trust in the Lord. Make up your mind that no matter what happens, no matter what comes, you will not fear; instead you will trust in God. It is your only defense against the unknown.

The Apostle Paul faced incredible odds and enormous trouble. But he too knew the only prescription that would work. That's what he meant when he said, "I also suffer these things: nevertheless I am not ashamed: for I know whom I have believed, and am persuaded that he is able to keep that which I have committed unto him against that day" (2 Timothy 1:12). That's trusting. . . that's facing trouble.

POWER THOUGHT

Since I do not know what tomorrow holds, I will trust him who holds tomorrow.

◆ 31 ◆
Time Out

When you are getting tired and your opponent is starting
to pull ahead, you feel as though you need a new
strategy. You're ready for a time out. A good coach knows
when to give his team a chance to breathe and when to
offer some suggestions. He also knows that a time out
often will interrupt the other team's rhythm and
momentum.

Used properly, time outs can be as productive in the
long run as going all out.

Many times you will get so weary you can hardly keep
going. You may feel that what you are doing isn't
working. Or, as someone put it, "The hurrieder I go, the
behinder I get."

When that happens to you, don't be afraid to call time
out in the game of life. We all need it from time to time.
Even Jesus went away from the multitudes to be alone, to
pray, to rest a while before going back to minister.

Take time out to rest. When you get tired, it's easy to
get confused, frustrated, and discouraged. You may
reach the point of not knowing what to do next, and be
too tired to care. Call time out! Stop and catch your
breath. The Lord says, "Be still, and know that I am God"
(Psalm 46:10). A little rest always makes you feel better
and see things more clearly. Spend a time out with God
and let him help you get your act back together.

Take time out to reflect. Sometimes a ball player is told
about a mistake he is making during a time out. This
correction is not intended as punishment. The coach
simply wants to help him do better so the team will win.
His comments are for illumination and instruction.

Remember that the changes God asks you to make in

your life are to make you a better player...a winner. The Bible says, "Happy is the man whom God correcteth" (Job 5:17). Why? "For whom the Lord loveth he chasteneth" (Hebrews 12:6). So during the time outs, be willing to learn from your mistakes.

Take time out to listen to the coach. When a basketball team calls a time out, the players don't scatter and do their own thing — they immediately huddle around the coach to hear what he has to say. They realize that his words are just as important as rest and refreshment.

During your time outs, read your Bible and let it speak to your heart. You will find that the Word of God will instruct you and inspire you as well. As you study the Scriptures, God will help you to replay your strategy in the game of life. "Trust in the Lord with all thine heart; and lean not unto thine own understanding. In all thy ways acknowledge him, and he shall direct thy paths" (Proverbs 3:5, 6).

POWER THOUGHT

The most important time you spend in your busy day is the time out you take to spend with God.

◆ 32 ◆
Catch Up and Stay Up

The best way to stay ahead is never to get behind. But every player eventually finds himself in a situation in which his team is behind and is forced to play "catch up." It's a tough act...and one you don't forget easily.

I can still remember in detail a lot of them. One I recall most clearly happened during my senior year at OCU. We were twelve points behind Miami, Florida's team, at the half. And to make it worse, the refereeing had to be the worst I had ever seen. One of their players shot thirty-four free throws! It was a real snake pit. It would have been easy to throw in the towel and give up in disgust.

But our coach kept telling us to stay with our game plan, do our thing, keep our cool. And that's what we did. We played as hard as we could, and finally tied the game at the buzzer. Then in overtime we won, 118 to 113. That win was more meaningful to our team than any of the games in which we led from the start and won by a wide margin.

Our coach always insisted that if we would apply a few basic principles we would win more than our share of the "catch up" games. First, he said, it won't happen fast. Hurried shots and rushed passes usually put you farther behind. Sure, the clock is running, but that's why you have to make every move count.

It's really a matter of staying in control. You don't get behind in one minute, and you can't expect to catch up in one minute. Work hard, but take the time you need to make your work count.

The same principle applies off the court. A friend of mine has a motto card in his workroom that I like a lot, especially for catch-up situations. It says simply, "If you don't have time to do it right, when will you have time to do it over?"

Second, use your time outs to refresh your mind and body, as well as for planning your strategy. Recall the plays and practices that will be useful for catch-up situations.

That's also a good strategy for Christian living. That's why I always recommend that Christians take time out of every day . . . to pray, meditate, read their Bible and listen for God's word for their life. Even when we feel as though we're behind in life, there's nothing that can help us cope better than the resources available to every Christian.

The third step in the art of catching up is never to give up. Like the tortoise in the famous fable, keep on keeping on even when it seems the hare has passed you by. He may become overconfident and sit down to rest. Do the very best you can, give all you've got, don't hold anything back. And remember, you usually catch up by the inch, not the yard.

Finally, don't despair when you get behind. You can catch up and you can still win. It probably won't happen all at once. You may need to take some time outs along the way. But if you refuse to give up, you can make it. And the victory will taste even better!

POWER THOUGHT

Take life one step at a time.

◆ 33 ◆
Don't Slow Down
Too Quickly

Many times teams that are well ahead go into what they call their delay game in the closing minutes of the final period. Essentially, they are trying to use up the clock by slowing down the pace, controlling the ball, and taking as much time as they can with each maneuver. They're really not interested in scoring any more points as long as they can keep their opponents from catching up.

While this strategy can be effective, I've seen teams end up losing because they went into the delay game too early. In fact, while I was writing this book I saw a perfect example. My daughter was playing for a junior high school team and I went to watch. The first half was disastrous for us. Nothing went right, and the score after two periods was 21-6.

But in the second half our team began to score and to catch up. When the other coach saw what was happening, he called for the delay game. But it was much too early for that. Our team managed to keep scoring and tied up the score 24-24 at the end of the third quarter.

It was the beginning of the end for the other team. They forgot that they had gotten ahead by running, shooting, and hustling. They kept trying to play their delay game. But they lost the ball; they walked; they stopped scoring.

In the end, we won by a score of 30-28.

As I sat in the stands watching, it occurred to me that many people make the mistake of trying to use the delay game in life . . . and end up losing. They start out well, trusting, believing, working hard and being productive. Then they see that they are doing okay, so they lay back and try to coast. That's when they start to lose.

Someone said the Christian life is somewhat like a bicycle in that you either go forward or you fall off. And they are so right. The Christian life is not designed for a delay game strategy. The fast break works much better! There is a world to win out there, and you can never accomplish that by standing around.

Yes, you need to take a time out to recuperate, regroup and plan your next series of plays. But then it's time to get back on the boards, to run and gun and go for it.

There may have been a time in your life when you were really warm toward the Lord — you walked with him and served him. But then you started trying to coast, and now you find that you've gotten cold and out of it.

Forget the delay game. Get back to the thick of it. Now is the time to begin pressing. Remember the advice of the apostle to the Hebrews: "Let us lay aside every weight, and the sin which doth so easily beset us, and let us run with patience the race that is set before us" (Hebrews 12:1).

POWER THOUGHT

I will win in life by striving to work as hard and run as fast at the end of the game as I did at the beginning.

◆ 34 ◆
Overtime

All coaches have their own version of the overtime speech. It usually comes after an extra-long, super-strenuous workout. Just about the time you expect to hear him say, "Hit the showers," he starts his speech.

First, he reminds you that if a game ends in a tie, there will automatically be a five-minute overtime period put on the official clock. "That means," he says, "the winning team will be the one that has something extra...the one that can reach down and pull out that added strength for victory."

By then you know what is coming — more wind sprints, ten more laps, up and down the steps five more times, then five minutes of hard scrimmage. You get the message. You're preparing for the overtime.

And the only way to be ready to play tough in overtime, even when you're tired, is to practice tough *when you're tired.* Then when the big game ends in a tie and the scoreboard clock flashes five more minutes, you will have the extra edge of confidence that comes from knowing you've been there before...and handled it.

The same thing applies to life's "overtime" experiences. It can be the death of a parent, a friend or loved one. You think you can't stand it. Or divorce rips your family apart and you feel lonely, bitter, and resentful. Maybe disappointment ruins everything you'd been working for and looking forward to. Any one of those is an "overtime" situation.

What do you do? How do you handle such a challenge? Especially when you're bone-weary and not functioning at your best?

Here are some guidelines that have worked for me in life's overtime experiences.

First, depend on God. Basketball players learn to look for the coach's signals and depend on his expertise during overtimes. And in the game of life, you must realize that God knows the road through your wilderness. Depend on him.

Second, depend on God's Word. The Bible is filled with examples of people who were faced with overtimes and came through on top. There are countless other references that can provide just the guidance or encouragement you need to keep on keeping on. Get acquainted with your Bible and mark those passages that could be helpful in the future. Then when you need them, they're right at your fingertips.

Third, depend on your fellow Christians, your spiritual team members. You are not alone. Share your distress with a friend who can pray with you and sustain you. In overtime situations it is wise to remember the "*I* can't; *we* can" formula. And even if all your teammates seem effectively screened off from you, remember that Jesus said, "I will never leave thee, nor forsake thee" (Hebrews 13:5).

Fourth, pray specifically about your problems, your overtime demand. Don't be ashamed to say, "I'm afraid. . .I'm depressed. . .I'm angry. . .I'm too tired." Be honest about your confusion or despair. Then ask for help. You'll get it.

One more thing: don't give up. Keep on going, moving, trying. This little verse sums it up well. It's called, "It's Easy to Quit."

It is easy to quit. Anyone can say
"The hill is too high" or "It's too far away."
Anyone can say, "I'm too tired to keep on,"
And stop halfway there. But don't be that one.
.Whenever life gives you a task to do,
Don't stop in the middle but see the thing through.
It's easy to quit. Any fool can explain
To himself and his friends why the struggle was vain.
It doesn't take brains when you start cutting loose
From a difficult task to think up an excuse.

"God is faithful, who will not suffer you to be tempted above that ye are able; but will with the temptation also make a way to escape, that ye may be able to bear it" (1 Corinthians 10:13).

◆ 35 ◆
We Beat Ourselves

Sooner or later it happens to every team. They walk off the court after the game muttering to themselves, "We blew it. We gave it away. They didn't beat us . . . we beat ourselves!"

There is no loss harder to take than the one you caused yourself. Bad passes, forced shots, lane violations, walking with the ball are all mistakes that can destroy you.

That's a lot different from being outplayed fair and square by a better team. In those situations you can still walk away with your head held high because you know you did your best. But it's a bitter pill to swallow when the game was yours for the taking and you let it get away . . . *you beat yourself.*

My experience with this kind of defeat has convinced me that nine times out of ten it's due to inadequate preparation, not working hard enough, being overconfident, or not taking an opponent seriously.

Many times it can be traced to the way a team practices. Sometimes players forget that even though team preparation is called practice, it's really a part of the game ahead. And the bad habits repeated on the practice court can carry over right into the game.

It can happen in life, as well. Lack of discipline and careless preparation can cause us to throw away our chance to be victorious. Or a bad attitude can result in our not doing our best; then when the test comes we are not ready. To twist a cliche, we snatch defeat from the jaws of victory.

Ignorance of God's Word can also trip us up. It is easy to put off reading the Bible and pass up letting the Holy

Spirit teach us and open our understanding. But constant exposure to the Word of God is one of the keys to victory. The psalmist declared, "Thy word have I hid in mine heart, that I might not sin against thee" (Psalm 119:11). And the wisdom of Solomon includes this solid information: "For thy commandment is a lamp; and the law is light; and reproofs of instruction are the way of life" (Proverbs 6:23).

Also it is never a good idea to underestimate your adversary. While you need not be afraid of the enemy, you should take him seriously and be prepared to face whatever attack he may launch against you. Peter wrote: "Be sober, be vigilant; because your adversary the devil, as a roaring lion, walketh about, seeking whom he may devour" (1 Peter 5:8).

Even so, there is no force Satan can bring against you that is strong enough to defeat you. With God's help and strength, you are invincible. You can, indeed, "do all things, through Christ" (Philippians 4:13). God has provided you with salvation.

He has given you access to his power.

You have been given the weapons ultimately to defeat any foe.

So, if you've been losing lately — beating yourself — then wake up, get in uniform, take your enemy seriously, and get yourself up for the battle. Go out in confidence, praying as though it all depended on God and working as though it all depended on you.

That way you'll be sure not to beat yourself!

POWER THOUGHT

"But thanks be to God, which giveth us the victory through our Lord Jesus Christ" (1 Corinthians 15:57).

◆ 36 ◆
Sidelined

The secret fear of every athlete is being sidelined with an injury. And it happened to me at the beginning of my senior year in high school.

One night I was driving toward the basket and a boy sped across the floor to block my shot. He didn't block the shot, he blocked me . . . and we both fell on the floor.

When I pushed him off me, I saw that my left hand was back up under my elbow. I got hold of the wrist with my right hand and put it back where it was supposed to be. Then, I went to the bench and said, "Coach, it's broken!"

Well, you know how optimistic basketball coaches are. He felt it and said, "It's just sprained — it's going to be okay."

But the doctor at the hospital said it was a compound fracture and he put my arm in a cast. The next day the newspapers reported it, saying our team had now lost its leading scorer.

A couple of weeks later at our first ball game, the coach asked me to lead in prayer before the team left the dressing room. This was the first time in a couple of years that I would not be going out to start the game. As I prayed I cried. I was hurt. I was disappointed.

I remember wondering what possible good could come out of a broken arm. I walked out of the dressing room to watch my teammates play without me. The tears streamed down my face as I sat on the bench. I was heartbroken.

But as I look back on that hurt and disappointment now, I thank God for what happened, because it was during that time that I felt God's call to be a minister.

In my disappointment, I found God's appointment for my life. I can honestly say that if it had not been for that injury I might not be preaching today. During a seeming defeat I discovered a win.

No wonder the Apostle Paul said, "Thanks be unto God, which *always* causeth us to triumph" (2 Corinthians 2:14).

In the years since that disappointment, so many times I've seen good come out of what seemed a total setback. The Bible explains it this way: "We know that all things work together for good to them that love God, to them who are the called according to his purpose" (Romans 8:28).

When disappointment strikes — the kind that hurts way down deep — we don't always remember this. All kinds of reactions set in. You say, "Why? This is the worst thing that's ever happened to me. I can't go on. Where in the world is God?"

I don't know what kind of disappointment you are facing today, what broken dream. Maybe it was something beyond your control, and it is destroying your will to fight, your courage, maybe even your will to live. But I've discovered this: if you'll give that disappointment to Christ, he'll bring forth purpose and meaning out of that seemingly meaningless hurt. He will work it into the total picture of your life.

The Bible says to cast all your care, all your disappointments, all your hurts on Christ, for he cares for you (1 Peter 5:7).

The psalmist said, "Commit thy way unto the Lord" (Psalm 37:5). Now that means your disappointments and your hurts. In other words, when disappointment comes, as quickly as you can get over the initial reaction, give it to God. Tell him, "I can't carry this. I don't understand why it happened." Then give it to Jesus. Don't nurse that thing that grieves you. Let the Lord take it from you and lift the load from your shoulders.

When you surrender it to him, you'll experience victory.

POWER THOUGHT

In the midst of every disappointment of life, you can find God's appointment.

◆ 37 ◆
Keep Walking

During my senior year in college one of the guards twisted his ankle, and it swelled to at least twice its normal size. It hurt so bad he knew it would be at least a month before he could walk on it again.

The doctor gave him a shot and said, "Start walking on it and it will get well."

At first he used crutches because he couldn't stand to put any weight on it. When he remembered what the doctor said, he started hobbling around, putting weight on it. Soon he was able to walk and to jog. It still hurt, but he kept going.

The team flew to Florida for a game soon afterward, and he got out and started running along the sand. The more he ran, the looser his ankle felt. The swelling began to go down. And after a few miles of running, he felt strong enough to play again.

If he had sat around with his foot up as he had intended to do, he would have been crippled for weeks. But by following the doctor's advice — even though it hurt — he was back in the game in just a few days.

There are lots of people who are going through life crippled because they don't want to go through the pain of growing. Are you crippled in your relationship with another person because you think it would be too painful to work out the strain? Do you have some habit that is crippling you spiritually and you're afraid it will hurt too much to walk away from it?

Let me encourage you to get up and step out right now. You can do it. God has given you the power to walk. . .to become strong and whole. One of my favorite verses says, "But as many as received him, to them gave he *power to become* the sons of God, even to them that believe on his name" (John 1:12).

Once Jesus came to a man who had been crippled for thirty-eight years. He was a defeated man who lay on a pallet near the Pool of Bethesda, encircled by other people who were also defeated, sick, tired, and crippled. He was a loser, surrounded by losers.

Jesus came to the man and asked, "Do you want to get well?"

The man began making excuses. "I've been this way for years. No one will help me."

And the Lord said, "Rise!" I believe Jesus was talking to the man on the inside. For a person never gets up on the outside until he first gets up on the inside.

Then the Master said, "Take up your bed and walk." You see, the man had been on the bed for thirty-eight years. The bed had been carrying the man. Now it was time for the man to carry the bed.

And he did! The Bible says, "And immediately the man was made whole, and took up his bed, and walked" (John 5:9).

What will you do today? Do you want to remain a cripple or do you want to walk? It's really up to you.

You can lie on your bed and squawk.
You can sit on your bed and talk.
Or you can take up your bed and walk.

Just like the man in the Bible, first of all you've got to want to be made whole. You've got to want to be a winner. Second, you must let Christ speak to your inner man. It may be your mind, your thinking, that is crippled the most. And third, you've got to stand up and start walking.

Oh, it may be tender at first — even painful. But keep walking. You may stumble a little, and go a bit slowly. But keep going. If you will receive him, Christ will give you power. And if you're willing to walk, he'll help you to run. Every step will be a stronger step until the thing that has crippled you falls away . . . and you are made whole.

POWER THOUGHT

"Rise, take up thy bed, and walk" (John 5:8).

◆ 38 ◆
Winning Is More Fun

Everybody likes to win — to be on a winning team.
When you're winning, the gym is full of fans and the air is
filled with cheers. The coach is a hero and the players
feel like they can conquer a giant. It is easy to smile and
face the public when you're winning. But winning is no
simple matter . . . for in every game one team will lose, no
matter how much the players wanted to win.

That's why I think winning is first of all a matter of
attitude. Despite what others may think or write, winners
know they have the capacity to win. Their winning
attitude is contagious. It infects others. It generates
enthusiasm. Enthusiasm creates excitement. Excitement
gives that extra edge that every winner must have.

Winning is also a matter of teamwork. Pity the poor
player who really believes he's so great a star that he can
do it all. Where would he be without the assists, the good
passes, the screening and hustle that let him benefit from
the play of others. The winning teams I've been on always
had a lot of players in double figures. Sure, there were
some who stood out in scoring, but they were balanced
by a strong team on the boards, in ball-handling and
discipline.

Winning is also a matter of luck . . . but not what you
normally think of as luck. I like the way Bobby
Rutherford, the great Indianapolis race car driver,
defined it. He said, "Luck is when opportunity meets
preparation." Nothing counts more to winners than
preparation. Frank Ramsey, the great All-American from
Kentucky and later with the Boston Celtics as a pro,
would go to the gym an hour before the game to *prepare*
mentally. He did that by meditating . . . psyching himself

up to play his best, to be *prepared* to grab the opportunity when it came.

Finally, winning is consistency. It's easy to let up after a tough game, or a great game. It's tempting to look past what should be an easy win to next week's big game. But the great player treats every game as one that requires his best. It's as if he were just starting a new season. I like the slogan, "Today is the first day of the rest of your life." Today's game can be the first game of the rest of your life. That approach will insure consistency and winnings throughout.

The Apostle Paul also talked about being a winner. He said, "I have fought a good fight, I have finished my course, I have kept the faith: Henceforth there is laid up for me a crown of righteousness" (2 Timothy 4:7, 8). He also knew it took hard work. "I press toward the mark for the prize of the high calling of God in Christ Jesus" (Philippians 3:14).

Never think that today's victory will bring a win tomorrow. Each game demands that you play to the best of your ability and give it all you've got. Just as a loser works to be a winner, a winner must keep on working. . . or become a loser.

You can go from mountaintop to mountaintop if you give your best. And in the Christian life, you can grow and grow if you do not try to live off past victories. Remember Paul's formula for winning. He said, "I press on" — not "I sit out."

POWER THOUGHT

Your first win came from preparation and hard work. Your next victory will come the same way. . . or not at all!

◆ 39 ◆
Losers Can Be Winners

Every player has heard the cliché, "It's not whether you win or lose that's important, but how you play the game." I've always thought that whoever said that had never played basketball, or he would know that winning and losing do make a difference (a very big difference indeed...especially if you lose).

I know because I've played a lot and lost a lot. Even though I was on some great teams, I know how terrible it is to walk off the court having lost.

It's heartbreaking to do your very best, strain to your very limit, and still come out on the short end of the score. And the more you lose, the worse it gets. It's hard to face the fans; it's difficult to keep up your enthusiasm.

Even if you're not a player, it can be tough to be loyal and supportive of a team that keeps on losing.

But that's how basketball and Christian living are different. When a basketball game is over and the other team finished ahead — that's it. You lost. But in living you can win even when it looks like you've lost.

That's the way it was with Jesus. A good example is found in one of my favorite Scripture verses, John 16:33. Just hours before Jesus was to be betrayed, when everything he had worked for seemed lost, when even his disciples would soon flee and deny him...Jesus had the audacity to say, "Be of good cheer, I have overcome the world."

Anyone else looking on would have laughed and said something like, "Hey, man! Open your eyes. You're finished...failed. The end is near."

But every Easter says different. Every reborn Christian says different. Jesus won even though it looked as if he had lost.

There is a great difference between not always winning and being a loser. The champion fighter may get hit many times — even knocked down. But he keeps getting up, and is not a loser until he stays down.

Losing one battle, or two, doesn't mean you've lost the war. It's only necessary to win one more than you lose to be a winner.

So don't give up — ever. You are on God's team and it has never been stopped! "If God be for us, who can be against us?" (Romans 8:31). I heard about a little boy who tried to quote that verse in Sunday school, and came out with, "If God is for you, everybody else might as well be!" And that's the truth.

POWER THOUGHT

There is a big difference between not always winning and being a loser! Don't give up.

◆ 40 ◆
On a Losing Streak?

No one likes to lose.

A losing streak is like a jinx. It's hard to break it. Your fans start losing interest and it's hard to play to empty seats. This is when discouragement sets in, and you need to know how to deal with it.

When a word starts with *dis,* it usually means that whatever comes after it has been lost. So *dis*couragement means the loss of courage, the loss of heart, the loss of the will to fight and win. A discouraged person is usually a defeated person. For whatever you have in your heart looks out through your eyes. And if you're discouraged within, more than likely as you look out on the world, everything will look discouraging and defeating to you. Victory will seem impossible.

Christ met some discouraged fishermen one day. They had fished all night long and caught nothing. They were sitting on the shore washing their nets, tired, glum, and cynical. The Lord said, "Cast your nets over on the other side of the boat and you'll catch fish."

Peter, the leader of the men, said "What's the use? We're tired. We've worked all night and haven't even seen a fish. Right now we're ready to throw in the towel and go home."

These fishermen were in a losing slump. Peter didn't think they needed to go to the trouble of trying even one more time. Then — he changed his mind.

"Nevertheless, Lord," he said, "at thy word I will let down the net. I will try again."

When you're discouraged, that's the time to change your mind about God, yourself, and your situation.

Christ came to the fishermen and said, "I understand

your problem. And I will help you right where you are."

If Christ didn't come to you and me where we are, he wouldn't come to us at all. He comes to you in the middle of a mess, in the midst of a trial, in the midst of trying and adverse conditions. And he says, "Don't quit. Try one more time. This time you're going to win."

When you can't seem to get out of a losing streak, quit arguing with the Lord. Change your mind as Simon Peter did. Say, "Nevertheless, Lord, at thy word I will try one more time." Give your losses to the Lord. This is what Peter did. And you know what happened!

When the nets were let down again, a great school of fish filled them up to the breaking point. Peter called to other fishermen to come help him. They caught so many fish that their boat started to sink under the load!

Can't you imagine the joy on the faces of Peter and the other fishermen? Their losing streak was broken. They had started winning again.

Your losing streak can be broken too. Just at the moment when you're ready to give up — just when you think you're not going to make it — Jesus will come to you at the point of your need. That's the moment to bury your discouragement and let your faith in God rise to the occasion.

POWER THOUGHT

Discouraged people don't see miracles coming. So don't give up. . . look up!

◆ 41 ◆
Instant Replay

Long before television developed the "instant replay" technique for sports spectators, athletes were using the process almost constantly.

Four hours after the game they lay in their beds, eyes wide open, rerunning each play of the game in their minds and asking, "Why didn't I do this instead of that?"

But no matter how many times you replay the game it always comes out the same. As one coach jokingly said to a friend, "I kept waiting for us to win on the replay. . . but we never did!"

Athletes aren't the only ones who have to contend with mental replays of their mistakes and losses. Every person who gets into the game of life soon discovers that the bitter memories of mistakes are about as bad as failure itself. You must learn to cope with "instant replays."

Here are some suggestions to help you get through those sleepless nights when every mistake you ever made plays itself over and over in your mind.

First, learn from your mistakes. An error in judgment or just a plain old clumsy blunder may have led to the loss of a game. But if you learn from the experience so that you won't make the same mistake again, it may lead to a victory tomorrow.

Second, forgive yourself. Since you can't do anything about it, stop punishing yourself. Forgive yourself and go on.

Third, forgive your teammates for their mistakes. Since you can't do anything about the past, forgive them and encourage them to get back into the game, doing their best.

Fourth, quit looking back and start looking forward to

the next game. You can't do anything about yesterday's loss but you can focus all your attention and direct all your energy on today's contest. Rehashing yesterday doesn't put you in a good frame of mind for today . . . or tomorrow. Remember the Apostle Paul's formula for success: "Forgetting those things which are behind, and reaching forth unto those things which are before . . ." (Philippians 3:13).

Fifth, focus on what you did that was right. You'll find that it is much more productive to emphasize the good parts of your game than to concentrate on not doing the bad things.

Sixth, forget the defeat. Put it out of your mind. As Paul said, if it's lovely and of good report, think about it. If it isn't, kick it out of your computer (Philippians 4). When God forgives your sins, he forgets them. You must do that too. Erase your instant replay tape and get back in the game.

POWER THOUGHT

"This one thing I do, forgetting those things which are behind, and reaching forth unto those things which are before, I press toward the mark for the prize of the high calling of God in Christ Jesus" (Philippians 3:13, 14).

◆ 42 ◆
The Length of the Game

A high school basketball game is thirty-two minutes long. A college game has forty minutes of playing time. And the game is not over until the last second has ticked off.

Some teams make the mistake of using themselves up in the first half. Before the second half is over, they have run out of gas and have to coast the rest of the way. If their opponent is still going strong, they probably will lose.

That's why a good coach prepares his team to play the full length of the game — not just the first half. He has a strategy for both halves of the game. He knows that wise pacing in the first half often produces victory in the second half. The game is not always won by the team that starts strongest.

The same principle is true in life. Unfortunately there are a lot of people who are using themselves up in the first half of life. A popular song recorded by Peggy Lee put it in the form of a question, "Is That All There Is?" It suggested that since everything else had been disappointing, maybe the thing to do was just keep on dancing and boozing until one got up the nerve to try death. In other words, play only the first half; end your life before it's really begun.

It's hard to believe, but this is exactly what is happening among a lot of teenagers. Suicide is their number two killer. Apparently they've come to the conclusion that there is nothing left worth living for.

I call this playing the second half before the first half is over. And it is a tragic waste. It comes from pushing too much in every stage of life. Children are pushed to dress, act and behave like teens. Teenagers are made to feel if they haven't tried everything by the time they reach high school they're hopelessly slow and "out of it." And if a college student doesn't step into a career that produces instant prestige and enough money to buy all the status symbols, he is looked on as a failure. In fact, all through life, men and women are constantly made aware of those who have made it bigger, better, and faster than they have.

But the game is not over until all the time on the clock has elapsed. The second half is just as important — probably more important — than the first half. Half time scores don't count.

When you get depressed or discouraged, don't give up. There's a lot more of life to live. In fact, there's another half at least. The score can change; you can change; situations can change — all for the better.

Two thousand years ago the Apostle Paul had something like that in mind in his letter to the Philippians (3:16) when he said, "Forgetting those things which are behind, and reaching forth unto those things which are before, I press toward the mark for the prize of the high calling of God in Christ Jesus." So must we.

POWER THOUGHT

Paul could say of his life: "I have fought a good fight, I have finished my course, I have kept the faith" (2 Timothy 4:7). And so can you . . . when you live your life for Christ.

◆ 43 ◆
The Last Game

I'll never forget playing my last college basketball game. Our team had traveled to Denton, Texas, to face North Texas State in the last game of the season.

I went into it with mixed emotions. I felt as if I had been playing basketball all of my life. It was part of me, and yet the time had come to lay it down. Not only would I not be playing anymore but I would be leaving a great coach and my teammates. After graduation we would go our separate ways and might never see each other again.

But there was something exciting about that last game. Perhaps one of the things that softened the blow for me was the knowledge that I had something to look forward to after it was over. The game was on Monday night . . . and I was to be married the following Saturday. When my last game was over I faced a new beginning!

The Bible teaches that this is the pattern of the game of life. There will be a last game . . . an ending. It is called death. The Scriptures say, "It is appointed unto men once to die" (Hebrews 9:27). On his deathbed, David explained to his son, "I go the way of all the earth" (1 Kings 2:2).

Death is inescapable. It will come to everyone without exception. David Ringer's book, *Looking Out for No. 1,* tells of a New York stockbroker who had amassed a personal fortune of more than fifty million dollars. Then he was stricken with a terminal disease. He declared bitterly, "Life has played a trick on me. All my plans and preparations were for living — I am not prepared for death."

Jesus said, "Let not your heart be troubled: ye believe in God, believe also in me. . . . I go to prepare a place for you . . . that where I am, there ye may be also (John 14:1–3).

You cannot avoid the last game. It will come. But you can be sure of being on the winning team, through faith in Christ. The outcome has already been decided. The final story has already been written. You can read it for yourself in 1 Corinthians 15:54, 55, 57. "Death is swallowed up in victory. O death, where is thy sting? O grave, where is thy victory? . . . thanks be to God, which giveth us the victory through our Lord Jesus Christ."

POWER THOUGHT

With Christ, I will win my last game. "The last enemy that shall be destroyed is death" (1 Corinthians 15:26).

◆ 44 ◆
My Friend's Last Game

While I was writing this book of devotionals, a good friend of mine and his wife played their last game. It was completely unexpected — a tragedy that shook our community.

Richard Douglas was pastor of a large Baptist church in Oklahoma City. Two men came to his door at about 9:15 one evening and asked to use the telephone. Once inside, they pulled out guns and robbed the house. Then they shot Richard, his wife Marilyn, and their two children. Only the children survived, after two weeks in intensive care at the hospital.

My daughter is the same age as the Douglas girl and they went to the same school. So the whole senseless, brutal attack hit us very hard. In addition to dealing with my own grief at the loss of a friend, I found myself needing to help my family cope with the questions this tragedy raised.

"Why did this have to happen?"

"Where are my friends' parents now?"

"Will we ever see them again?"

Perhaps there never are enough concrete answers to settle every question that comes to mind during a time of suffering or loss. There are some things that will be answered only in eternity.

Interestingly enough, in the last sermon Richard Douglas preached, he declared he was ready to meet God whenever his time came. Unknown to him, that time was only hours away. During his funeral, those words from his last message were played. The news media picked them up and broadcast them all over the state and across the nation. Richard Douglas gave a testimony that he was ready for the last game.

Unfortunately, we don't know when that will be for us — no matter our age, or health, or how careful we are. Our last game can be anytime.

When I was at a crusade in Tuttle, Oklahoma, a few years ago, a whole group of young people were headed out of town to watch a drag race. A part broke on a pickup truck carrying two boys. They smashed into a telephone pole. One was killed instantly; the other died in the hospital.

They were young, healthy, happy. They thought they had lots of time to live, and to get ready to die.

When those young people came to my crusade services they were stunned and shocked at seeing death strike so close to home. They came with many questions. More than 100 made their decision for Christ. They decided the last game might be closer than they had ever realized. For that game they needed Jesus Christ in their hearts and lives.

Whatever your situation is, be sure you've prepared for life's last game. Ask Christ into your life now . . . while there's time.

POWER THOUGHT

"Yea, though I walk through the valley of the shadow of death, I will fear no evil, for thou art with me" (Psalm 23:4).

◆ 45 ◆
The Game after the Last Game

He starts out bouncing a ball on the driveway, or playing with the other kids at school. Then he learns enough and gets good enough to play on an organized team.

He makes the junior high team. . .and is promoted.

He makes the high school team. . .and is promoted.

Perhaps he even makes the team at his college or university, and works his way up to be on the starting five. And he is promoted to. . .?

Is he good enough to turn professional? Or to become a coach? Or simply to relive his moments of glory in the lives of his own children?

Ultimately the day comes when you can't keep up any longer. You can't jump as high. Your feet are not as quick. Your mind still knows what to do, but when it says *go there,* it takes too long for the rest of you to catch up. Your body starts slowing down.

When I was in high school and college I heard guys twice as old as I am say, "The first thing to go is your legs. Then you know you've got to quit." I'd laugh to myself and think, "It won't happen to me." But it did. Now, twenty years later, I still play for fun, but I understand full well what those "old guys" were talking about.

Sooner or later the day comes when you go from the court to the stands — when you take that little walk from the participants' arena to the spectators' place on the sidelines.

But life goes on — even though you find yourself in a place of transition and change, facing the unknown and the unfamiliar.

You need God then just as much as you did before. When you were in the game before, you were confident, experienced and ready. Now at this new level, you're not so sure. But just as the rewards and satisfaction increased as you moved from one level of playing competition to the next, so the fulfillment you need in this new area of challenge will come.

Just as you came to respect the coach's decision to put you in or take you out of the basketball games you played, so it's time to trust God's judgment of how and where to use you in the game of life. There is a game to be played. And there is a position only you can fill. So trust in God's strategy as your new game begins. Take each day as a gift from him. . .each opportunity as one provided especially for you. And live in the full knowledge of God's care and concern.

POWER THOUGHT

God intends to keep me in the game forever. "For I know the thoughts that I think toward you, saith the Lord, thoughts of peace, and not of evil, to give you an expected end" (Jeremiah 29:11).